BLACK'S PICTURE INFORMATION BOOKS

Scientific Adviser Jean Imrie MSc

prehistoric animals

DAVID SEYMOUR

Adam and Charles Black · London

Published by A & C Black Ltd
4, 5 & 6 Soho Square, London W1V 6AD

ISBN 0 7136 1412 9 (Limp)
      0 7136 1479 x (Boards)

First published in the Netherlands by Moussault's Uitgeverij NV under the title *Levensvormen uit het verleden* with a text by Dr G E de Groot; translated by Adrienne Dixon and comprehensively adapted by David Seymour with the assistance of Jean Imrie.

Filmset by Photoprint Plates Ltd, Rayleigh, Essex
Printed in the Netherlands by Ysel Press, Deventer

Acknowledgements

The drawings are by B Collet and J Timmers, and the colour transparencies are reproduced by permission of the Royal Museum of Geology and Mineralogy in Leiden. Black and white illustrations are as follows: Bruce Coleman Ltd 17; Mary Evans Picture Library 10; Geological Survey 8, 20; National Coal Board 7; Popperfoto 9.

Contents

A sabre-tooth tiger

Prehistoric animals

The plants and animals which inhabit the earth today are the descendants of forms of life which existed in the past. They are the products of a development which has gone on for millions and millions of years. The succession of various forms of plants and animals is known fairly well only over the past 500 million years; throughout that time we still have large gaps in our knowledge. 500 million years is only about an eighth or a tenth of the total history of the earth, which has existed for at least 4000 million years.

It is just as difficult for us to image 500 000 000 years as 4 000 000 000 years. Compared with these vast ages, man has been on earth for a very short time. Man-like creatures, called *Australopithecus,* first appeared about $2\frac{1}{2}$ million years ago. The earliest traces of life are a thousand times older—dating from some 2500 million years ago.

Determining the age of layers of the earth is a complicated business. The method is based on the existence of radio-active substances in some minerals. Radio-active elements are unstable, and they gradually change into stable substances. For example, a quantity of uranium will, after 4500 million years be only half its original size; the rest will have fallen apart and become lead and the gas helium. By measuring the amount of radio-active substance and the amount of end-product (for example how much uranium and how much lead) we can calculate how long it is since the mineral was formed.

Fossil fern in coal

Fossils

Almost all our knowledge of the appearance of past forms of life comes from fossils, which are the remains of plants and animals which lived on earth in the distant past. In most cases these remains consist of the hard shell or skeleton which the organism built up during its life—the shell of an ammonite or a snail, the skeleton of a coral polyp or the branch of a tree—but there are other forms of fossil which may occur (see illustrations 5–9).

Fossil-bearing cliffs on the north-east coast of England

The soft parts of an animal disintegrate soon after death. The flesh rots if it is not first eaten by scavengers. The hard parts will also disintegrate after some time if they remain exposed to destructive forces. One way in which they may be protected is if they are covered by a thin layer of silt. Silt consists of particles of sand, lime or clay, or some combination of these. The finer the particles of silt, the better the protection.

Silt is deposited, layer by layer, in water. From these layers of silt a fossil-containing rock will in time be formed. We still would not know much about the fossils if the rock remained on the sea-bed, but in the course of time there have been many periods of mountain formation. The rocks which were laid in regular layers on the sea-bed have been folded or pushed on top of one another, and later perhaps raised bodily until they formed the top of the highest mountains. Mighty mountain chains, such as the Rocky Mountains, the Alps and the Himalayas, were formed from rocks laid down on ocean floors in the remote past.

In many countries fossil-containing rock is exposed on the surface. Some areas of every country are famous for the number or quality of the fossils found there.

For a long time people thought of fossils as curiosities of nature. They were placed in collections of other curiosities. Towards the end of the eighteenth century, the English surveyor William Smith noticed that certain types of fossil were related to particular kinds of rock. He came to the conclusion that rocks could be described by means of the fossils they contained.

Geologists have since investigated the order of rock layers and given names to groups of rocks which seemed to be related by their nature and their fossil contents. In this way the 'geological time-scale' was drawn up, on which the relative age of various rocks can be indicated. At first it was impossible to put dates to this calendar—only the order was known. Now it is possible to add dates, though these cannot be precisely accurate. The geological time-scale is shown on page 24.

Slowly people came to understand that the plant and animal forms of the past had not changed suddenly, but gradually. There were often fossils which showed a transitional or intermediate form, between an earlier form and a later form. This was a confirmation of the theory of evolution, which assumes that one species may slowly develop out of another. Charles Darwin, who had collected over-whelming evidence in his book *The Origin of Species* (published 1859) to show that evolution had occurred, mentioned the lack of information about palaeontology. Palaeontology is the study of ancient plant and animal forms, many of which are now extinct.

A coelacanth—long thought extinct until one was caught by a fisherman

A cartoon, making fun of Darwin's theories, which are now accepted

The origin of life on earth

How did life start? People used to believe, and many still do believe, that this was a supernatural event. Some believe word for word the story of the creation as told in the Bible. Today more and more people wonder whether the origin of life, like the continuation of life, can be the result of a natural process.

We have no information about the first forms of life. However, we do think we know something about the conditions on earth when these forms evolved, about 3000 million years ago. Astronomers think that the atmosphere at that time consisted of helium, hydrogen, methane and ammonia gases. A similar mixture is found in the atmospheres of Jupiter and Saturn. The earth's atmosphere now, a mixture mainly of nitrogen and oxygen, could only have developed when plant forms had evolved which produced oxygen on a large scale. This process would have taken at least a thousand million years.

In the primitive atmosphere oxygen did not occur as a separate element (it appeared in compounds such as water vapour and carbon dioxide) and there was no layer of ozone in the atmosphere. Nowadays a layer of ozone screens the earth from the strong ultra-violet rays of the sun, but in ancient times these rays were able to penetrate the earth.

Experiments show that organic substances, the 'building blocks' of living creatures, can be formed from a mixture of methane, ammonia and hydrogen, in water and under the influence of electric discharges or strong ultra-violet radiation. A condition for this to occur is that there must be no free oxygen present.

Large amounts of organic substances could have been formed at that time, and for perhaps as much as a thousand million years they were able to accumulate in the water masses. It has been called 'the original organic broth'. In this organic 'soup' actual living cells may have formed, cells which were able to multiply themselves. But just how from the disordered mass of organic material an orderly cell structure could develop, is a question to which there is as yet no accepted answer. This is one of the most fascinating areas of contemporary scientific research.

The first traces of life

No remains of the earliest forms of life have been found, and it is most unlikely that they ever will be. These very early forms could have been small balls of soft protoplasm. The chances of any remains being left are minimal. Moreover, deposited rocks of that immense age are rarely exposed on the earth's surface and, where they are, they have almost always been distorted or changed by heat or pressure since they were deposited.

The oldest indications of life are, we think, about 2500 million years old. Chalk deposits of that age could have been formed by primitive blue–green algae. These can withstand ultra-violet light better than most organisms. But the plants themselves are not preserved, so it is pure guesswork that they were blue-green algae. The first undisputed remains are about 1500 million years old, and these *are* algae. It is not surprising that the oldest remains are those of plants. Plants must have developed long before animals; until there was sufficient oxygen dissolved in the water, animal life was impossible. Animals in fact, have always been dependent on the existence of plants, for food as well as for oxygen.

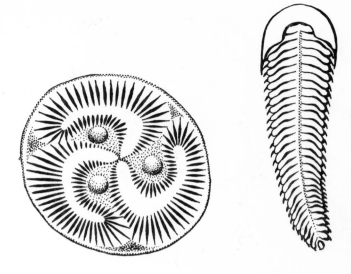

These were two forms of life which existed in the Pre-Cambrian period. Left: an animalcule of an unknown family, about 2 cm across. Right: a worm-like creature, 3 cm long

How animals developed is unknown, because fossil animals only appear from about 600 million years ago, in the rocks of the upper Pre-Cambrian. Even then, animal fossils are rare, though the variety of forms suggests that they had been evolving for some time. They include relatives of jellyfish, worms and echinoderms (see page 13). Many of them lacked hard parts. Some scientists think that animals evolved fairly late in the Pre-Cambrian, when there was already enough oxygen to make animal life possible on a large scale.

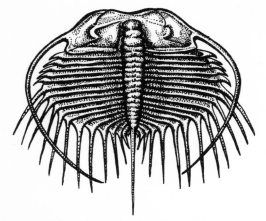

Shell of a trilobite from the Cambrian, about 2 cm long. Trilobites were one of the dominant forms of animal in the seas over a huge period of about 300 million years. Their armour did not grow with them, and they had to discard it several times during their lives, much as crabs do now

Towards the beginning of the Cambrian, most of the animal groups then living began to produce hardened body parts. Each group had its own method; one formed a shell of calcium, another a skeleton of silicon, another a 'coat' of chitin (a horn-like substance).

Developments were very gradual, taking thousands, even hundreds of thousands, of years. It is one of the riddles of palaeontology why all sorts of animals began more or less at the same time to build up hardened parts. We can only guess; perhaps as the seas became more populated, some animals began to prey on others with soft bodies. Yet jellyfish never joined this race to develop a skeleton; their defence against predators is their stinging cells.

Whatever the cause of the race, there are many more fossils from this period as a result. It is from this period that our knowledge, as opposed to guesswork, about the evolution of animals begins.

Evolution

Evolution does not always progress at the same pace. There have been times of 'rapid' development—rapid compared with other processes; the rapid developments still took thousands of years. Times of rapid development often follow periods of great mortality. If one species is dying out, another will take its place. If, when a new opportunity or a new environment presents itself, a few deviant forms appear which are better able to adapt to that environment, the deviant forms will begin to predominate with each succeeding generation. They are the animals most likely to reach adulthood, and so the most likely to reproduce themselves. This is what is meant by 'survival of the fittest'.

Cambrian

570–500 MILLION YEARS AGO. NAMED AFTER CAMBRIA, THE LATIN NAME FOR WALES. SEE ALSO PAGE 28.

In the seas of the Cambrian almost all groups of invertebrates (animals without backbones) were already present, in quite well-developed forms. An important animal at this time was the trilobite; its surviving relatives today are shrimps and lobsters. The part of trilobites which is preserved in fossil form is the external skeleton—a shield over the back consisting of chitin and calcium. The name 'trilobite' refers to the clear division of this shield into three parts or lobes. Trilobites are very useful as *zone fossils*: each of the different types of trilobite existed for a relatively short period, and was found in many parts of the world, so they can give a clear indication of the age of the rock layer in which they are found.

Shells of a present day and of a Cambrian brachiopod, about 1 cm wide

Apart from the trilobites, which became extinct at the end of the Permian, there were animals in the Cambrian seas whose descendants are still alive today. Jellyfish and sponges, shrimp-like creatures and brachiopods, all remain very similar to their remote ancestors. Snails and shellfish, on the other hand, now look very different from the molluscs of Cambrian times, and some echinoderms (modern examples are starfish and sea urchins) have also changed considerably.

Ordovician

500–440 MILLION YEARS AGO. CALLED AFTER THE ORDOVICES, AN ANCIENT CELTIC TRIBE. SEE ALSO PAGE 29.

Life was still restricted to water, both salt and fresh. The shallow seas had a rich variety of invertebrates. Trilobites flourished but no longer dominated. More and more animals developed a calcium skeleton or shell. Most Cambrian brachiopods, for example, had a shell of calcium phosphate, but Ordovician brachiopods mainly had shells of calcium carbonate. Corals and moss animalcules were common. Of the echinoderms, sea-lilies (crinoids) were widespread, but starfish were rare.

The molluscs began to look more like our snails and shellfish, but there were also nautiloids (illustrations 13 and 14) which have since declined, and are now represented by only one species. At that time some were over 4 metres long. They were the only predators in the Ordovician seas, and it may be that the appearance of these active hunters led to the development of defensive shells in other animals. Animals with shells would have had a better chance of survival.

Graptolites (iilustrations 13 and 16) were small animals with a skeleton of chitin, living together in colonies. They lived in tube-shaped shells, arranged along a stick. Several sticks might be bundled together under a bubble which kept them afloat. Graptolites are found all over the world, especially in black shales where they look like white lettering. They underwent a swift evolutionary development and became extinct after the Silurian.

Scales of fish are found from this period, and these are the first remains of vertebrates we have. The backbone may have been of cartilage rather than bone, however. The fragmentary remains do not tell us much about them.

A graptolite colony with a swimming bubble. The 'sticks' were about 4 cm long

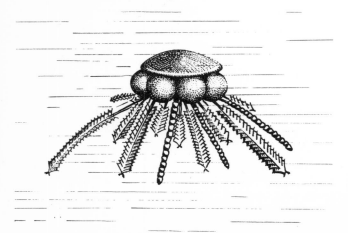

Silurian

440–395 MILLION YEARS AGO. NAMED AFTER THE SILURES, AN ANCIENT BRITISH TRIBE. SEE ALSO PAGE 30.

No drastic changes took place in the invertebrate animals, though some became more dominant, for example the eurypterids or 'sea scorpions' (see illustration 15 on page 30). But towards the end of the Silurian, the fishes (the first vertebrates) began to develop. Mostly they were jawless fish which could not grasp or chew their food, so they could not eat other animals or water-plants. Instead they crawled along the bottom of pools and rivers, filtering the silt and eating anything organic they found in it. Their gills served as sieves, as well as for breathing. Nowadays there are still two jawless fish, lampreys and hagfish. These are unable to grasp their food, but have developed sucker-like mouths so that they can suck blood from their prey.

The early jawless fish had a hard outer skeleton, but their internal skeleton was probably made of cartilage, as shark skeletons are today. (Babies' skeletons are made of cartilage, and we have cartilage between joints, for example in the knee.) Fossil jawless fish are found into the Devonian, but soon they were ousted by their descendants which had jaws, and were therefore better equipped for obtaining food.

A major development occurred during the Silurian which did not immediately affect animals. The first land plants appeared, with veins for the transport of water and mineral salts from their roots to the rest of the plant. Until plants had made this breakthrough on to dry land, it was impossible for animals to do so.

Devonian

395–345 MILLION YEARS AGO. NAMED AFTER DEVONSHIRE, THE ENGLISH COUNTY. SEE ALSO PAGE 32.

In the Devonian seas lived a multitude of invertebrates, including corals, trilobites, brachiopods, nautiloids, and a new relative of the nautiloids, the ammonite. Like the nautiloids, ammonites formed a shell made of calcite and divided into chambers. The chambers were attached to the inner side of the shell by more supports than in the case of the nautiloids. This is how the complicated patterns of suture lines were formed. Ammonite shells were stronger than those of the nautiloids.

In the Devonian, fishes developed considerably. The jawless fish were less common, and a rich variety of armoured fish with jaws evolved (illustrations 20–21). Many armoured fish spent their lives crawling along the beds of lakes or seas, but a number were more or less skilful swimmers. Whilst most grew to no more than 90 cm, there were some giants as long as 9 metres. With their huge jaws they must have been fearsome monsters to their smaller relatives. Most of the armoured fish became extinct towards the end of the Devonian, though a few continued into the Permian.

All groups of modern fish began their development during the Devonian: cartilaginous fish

A giant armoured fish, up to 9 metres long

(i.e. those with cartilage skeletons, such as sharks and skate), ray-finned fish (most of our present day fish), and the brush-finned fish, which are only sparsely represented now by the lungfish and coelacanth. The brush-finned fish are an important link in the development of vertebrates, because they were probably the ancestors of the amphibians, which were the first vertebrates to spend part of their lives on dry land. These fish had lungs, and the amphibians developed legs from fins.

The oldest known amphibian was found in late Devonian rocks; it still had fish characteristics. The climate at this time seems to have often included drought in high summer, which would have led to streams and lakes drying up. A fish with the ability to breath air directly through lungs, and to crawl to another pool which had not dried up, had a huge advantage for survival. This was probably how the amphibians developed.

During the Devonian, plant life on land had become richer and more varied. Insects had certainly appeared, and may well have begun to colonise the land.

Carboniferous

345–280 MILLION YEARS AGO. THE NAME MEANS 'COAL-BEARING'. THIS WAS WHEN MOST OF THE COAL DEPOSITS WERE FORMED. SEE ALSO PAGE 35.

The coal beds of western Europe were formed as peat in vast marshes during the Carboniferous. Some of the plant families of Carboniferous times are still represented today, but modern lycopods (club-mosses) and horsetails are very small compared with their tree-size ancestors. Lycopods grew up to 30 metres tall. Ferns with spores and also ferns with seeds were common.

The animals living in the marshes included arachnids, insects and amphibians of many varieties. The amphibians looked nothing like newts and frogs, but like them they started as water creatures in the larval stage, and their lungs and legs developed later. The eggs would have dried out on land, so they had to be laid in water.

The oldest known amphibian, Icthyostega, *found in Devonian rocks in Greenland, up to 90 cm long*

B Collet

The first reptiles appeared during the Carboniferous, making an enormous step forward with the development of a shell for their eggs. They could be laid on land without drying out. Many intermediate forms between amphibians and reptiles have been found, making the development clear. These early reptiles were insect-eaters. Since their descendants include birds as well as modern reptiles, you can see how significant the egg-shell turned out to be.

Permian

220–225 MILLION YEARS AGO. NAMED AFTER THE PROVINCE OF PERM IN THE URALS. SEE ALSO PAGE 36.

Many groups of plants and animals became extinct in this period. Trilobites, eurypterids, armoured fish and seed ferns all became extinct, and other groups were drastically reduced in numbers. 75% of the amphibian families and 80% of the old reptiles were extinct by the end of the Permian.

Such large-scale mortality is not uncommon in the history of the earth. It has been suggested that these forms of life had become too specialised, and were unable to deal with a suddenly changed environment. But the question remains, what were those changes which made life impossible both for land animals and plants and for many water dwellers? Why were other similar forms unaffected?

During the Permian there had been changes in sea level, with lakes and inland seas drying out, and this would affect water dwellers and possibly plants which needed damp conditions. Climatic changes could have affected plants, and the disappearance of plants would then affect animals. But in fact most plant groups continued to thrive in the Permian. The great mortality remains unexplained.

Meanwhile, there were many amphibians and reptiles, both plant-eaters and meat-eaters. Most lived near water, on the banks of pools and rivers. Both amphibians and early reptiles moved with difficulty on land, because their legs were placed more or less at the side of their body rather than underneath. Their way of walking was rather like that of a tortoise today. In fact the turtle family made its appearance in the next period, the Triassic, at about the same time as the dinosaurs. The turtle's amazing armour made it impossible, and unnecessary, for it to evolve more effective legs for use on land.

Fairly soon a group of reptiles developed which could walk more easily, with more slender bones and legs placed beneath the body. Their skeletons had features which resemble those of mammals and they are called pelycosaurs and therapsids.

This tortoise has survived a forest fire

A very early reptile, about 1·5 metres long

Triassic

225–150 MILLION YEARS AGO. THIS PERIOD DIVIDES NEATLY INTO THREE PARTS IN GERMAN GEOLOGY, WHICH IS HOW IT GOT ITS NAME. SEE ALSO PAGE 37.

After the large-scale mortality at the end of the Permian, there was a rapid development to fill up the spaces which had been left. The invertebrates on the sea beds underwent big changes: a new group of corals appeared, but moss animalcules, brachiopods and sea lilies had all suffered greatly, and ammonites only just survived. From the few ammonite species which were left, numerous new groups evolved.

There were fewer amphibians in the Triassic. They were no match for their descendants the reptiles, though some new amphibian forms developed in environments where they were not in direct competition, for example the frog.

Numerous new reptile groups developed, including turtles and crocodiles, as well as the first true lizards.

The pelycosaurs and therapsids continued to do well, and spread throughout the world. Their mammalian characteristics became more significant, and at the end of this period there were animals which showed characteristics of both reptiles and mammals.

Reptiles had developed as land animals, but some returned to life in the sea. Icthyosaurs or 'fish lizards' appeared, which must have been strong swimmers, and there were also plesiosaurs—reptiles with small heads, long necks and strongly developed paddle feet, which lived near the coast on a diet of fish. In the Triassic they were quite small, though their descendants grew to an enormous size. Their close relatives were animals which lived near the shores eating brachiopods and molluscs (page 37).

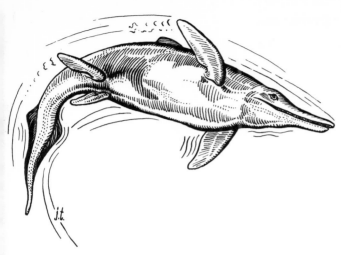

An icthyosaur, about 2 metres long

Jurassic

190–136 MILLION YEARS AGO. NAMED AFTER THE
JURA MOUNTAINS. SEE ALSO PAGE 38.

Towards the end of the Triassic and at the
beginning of the Jurassic, the climate deterior-
ated. The sea level also rose, and vast stretches
of land became shallow seas. This naturally
affected which animals flourished and which
died out.

The seas covering most of Europe teemed with
life; the fossils of this period give evidence of
this, and they are often very well preserved.
Ammonites had been through another difficult period, but now flourished once again and
developed many new forms. Icthyosaurs became completely adapted to life in the sea;
their bodies became streamlined, rather like

that of a shark or dolphin, though they are
not related to these animals. Sometimes two
completely independent lines of evolution
reach a similar climax—in this case the most
effective shape for a swimming animal of that
size.

On land the dinosaurs were the most spectacu-
lar, especially the huge predator dinosaurs and
the gigantic plant-eaters (illustration 35). Dinosaurs included some quite small, supple animals, as well as monsters like Tyrannosaurus
and Brontosaurus.

*Archaeopteryx, the oldest known bird, first appeared
during the Jurassic*

Reptiles during the Jurassic were lords of the sea and of the land, and they also became the first vertebrates to fly. The flying reptiles or pterosaurs had a broad wing of skin supported on the fourth finger of their fore-leg, which could almost be called an arm.

This type of structure was not followed up by later flying vertebrates. The oldest known bird, very rarely found as a fossil except in one particular quarry, also lived in the Jurassic. Archaeopteryx is a transitional form between reptiles and birds, and is counted as a bird because it has feathers. It is not directly derived from the flying reptiles.

Cretaceous

136–65 MILLION YEARS AGO. THE NAME MEANS 'CHALKY'. THE CHALK HILLS OF SOUTHERN ENGLAND WERE FORMED IN THIS PERIOD. SEE ALSO PAGE 41.

During the Cretaceous the plant life changed considerably, and this affected animal life. 'Modern' plants including flowering species, grasses and trees, began to take over from the ferns and horsetails. Leaves, seeds and berries provided a new kind of food for plant-eaters.

In the Cretaceous the reptiles had their heyday. There had never been such variety before. The

Typical chalk hills in southern England

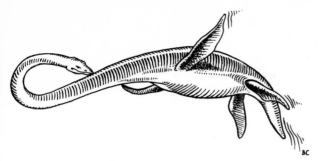

A paddling sea-reptile—the plesiosaur, up to 15 metres long

mild climate, with few changes in temperature, suited the cold-blooded animals and the luxuriant vegetation provided much food for the plant-eaters, including the horned dinosaurs, which appeared in the late Cretaceous (illustration 36). Turtles and crocodiles too were represented by more families than today.

Mammals had existed for 100 million years already as small, insignificant animals which kept out of the way of the reptiles. Now they began to evolve successful new lines. Marsupials developed, though they became isolated in South America and Australia. So did the ancestors of most present-day mammals, including the insect-eaters, of which we now have the mole, hedgehog and shrew.

Sea covered much of Britain and Europe; the invertebrates continued little changed. Boned fish went through a period of unprecedented development and they managed to outnumber the sharks in the seas. There were some reptiles hunting for fish. The icthyosaurs were less common, but a new group, the mosasaurs, appeared (illustrations 37 and 38).

Towards the end of the Cretaceous many groups became extinct. Belemnites and ammonites disappeared from the sea, this time for good. So did all the sea-reptiles except the turtle. The mosasaurs had been flourishing and their end came suddenly. 'Suddenly' does not mean overnight, but over many thousands, even hundreds of thousands, of years. This was still sudden compared with the icthyosaurs, for example, which were in decline for millions of years.

On land all the dinosaurs and flying reptiles disappeared, as well as many groups of tortoises and crocodiles. Again, we do not know what caused this great mortality. Why should so many animals become extinct when other animals with similar ways of life survived? No satisfactory answer, covering all the types of creature, has yet been suggested.

Tertiary

65–2 MILLION YEARS AGO. SCIENTISTS HAVE ABANDONED THE TERMS 'PRIMARY' AND 'SECONDARY' TO DESCRIBE OLDER PERIODS, BUT THE TERTIARY AND QUATERNARY HAVE BEEN LEFT! SEE ALSO PAGE 44.

The mammals developed enormously to take the places left by the dinosaurs and other reptiles. Whales and seals took the place of the sea-reptiles, and on land mammals took up their present dominant position. Early Tertiary mammals were small, with short legs, a small head and teeth that were not yet very specialised. Now very different forms began to

A primate of the Late Tertiary period, about 1 metre tall

develop—elephants, rats, whales, monkeys, camels, rabbits, cats, dogs, cows. Other forms appeared and became extinct during the Tertiary itself. For example, the odd-toed ungulates included many more families than those of the tapir, rhinoceros and horse which now represent the group.

The history of the horse family is well-known, thanks to a huge number of fossil finds (illustration 43). The history of the development of primates, leading to man, is far less well known. The primate group includes monkeys, apes and man, as well as their ancestors.

At the beginning of the Tertiary, when they appeared, the primates were similar to their insect-eating mammal ancestors, but they followed a different way of life and became adapted to living in trees. There they developed into nimble animals able to clutch branches with both hands and feet. Their long tails helped them to balance. The skull changed considerably; the eyes came closer together, so that the fields of vision in right and left eye overlapped, making three-dimensional vision possible. Very significantly, the skull increased in size as did the brain itself, and 'progress' in the primates is measured by the size of the brain in later specimens.

There are still great gaps in our knowledge of primate development; animals which live in trees have a poor chance of being preserved as fossils.

Quaternary

2 MILLION YEARS AGO TO THE PRESENT DAY. THE 'FOURTH PERIOD', FOLLOWING ON FROM THE TERTIARY. SEE ALSO PAGE 48.

During this period there have been severe fluctuations in climate, including several Ice Ages when the temperature was so low that land ice reached as far south as southern England, as well as large mountain ice caps round the Alps, Pyrenees etc. In between there were warmer periods, with higher temperatures than we have today. When the ice caps expanded, the sea level fell and shallow seas dried out. As the ice melted the sea level rose again, flooding valleys which had been inhabited by land animals.

living in the tundra plains included giant deer and woolly rhinoceros. Many of the large land mammals which had survived the cold became extinct a few thousand years ago. There is disagreement about the extent to which man may have caused this.

In the Quaternary, the youngest primate to develop was man. Fossil remains are found only rarely and after long searching. However, enough teeth, skulls and other parts of skeletons have been found to make our knowledge of man's family tree reasonable though not good. Remains of fossil primates are often too incomplete for scientists to say whether they are ape remains or human remains.

If tools, or stones which show signs of having been worked, are found near the site of the fossil, we can assume we are dealing with man. Only man makes tools. Much of our information about early Stone Age man comes from his tools, not from fossils.

In the middle of the Ice Ages, about 500 000 years ago, appeared the first people of our own kind, *Homo sapiens*. Physically man has evolved very little since that time. The size of the human brain has not increased over that time. What man has done with that brain is of course a different matter.

A giant deer. The span of the antlers was 3 metres

These variations of climate and sea level caused fairly rapid changes in the distribution of animals. Some animals could withstand the cold because of their fur or hair, for example the mammoth (illustration 44). Other animals

Geological time-scale

millions of years ago

		WATER	LAND
0			
	QUATERNARY		Development of man
100	TERTIARY		Rapid development of mammals
	CRETACEOUS	Last of the ammonites; sea-reptiles and boned fish thrive	Many groups of reptiles become extinct; flowering plants and trees prosper; heyday of the dinosaurs
	JURASSIC	Ammonites flourish	First mammals appear; oldest known bird
	TRIASSIC	Sea-reptiles first develop	Large groups of amphibians become extinct
200	PERMIAN	Trilobites, eurypterids and armoured fish become extinct	Reptiles thrive
	CARBONIFEROUS	Corals, brachiopods and sea-lilies thrive	Appearance of first reptiles; insects increase in number
300	DEVONIAN	Graptolites become extinct; considerable development of fishes	Oldest known amphibians; land plants become more luxuriant
400	SILURIAN	Jawless fish increase in number; eurypterids prosper	Oldest known land plants
	ORDOVICIAN	Oldest known fishes; graptolites flourish; nautiloids increase	
500	CAMBRIAN	Trilobites dominate the sea; almost all groups of invertebrates are represented	
600	PRE-CAMBRIAN		

Fossilisation

The fossils on this page consist of the hard parts of the organism.

1. Shell of ammonite in clay
Jurassic, 7 cm in diameter.

2. Moss animalcule colony in limestone
Cretaceous period, about 20 cm across. Usually each animalcule is less than a millimetre long.

3. Snail-shells in sandstone
Each shell is about 5 cm long.

4. Twig of a conifer in shale
Permian, 25 cm long.

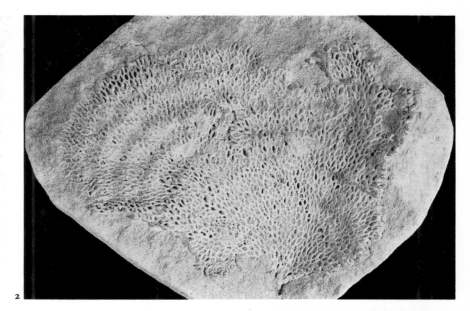

2

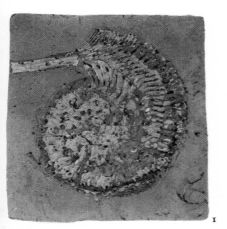

1

3

4

5. Stone core of an ammonite

The calcite shell has dissolved, but not until after the silt which has filled the hollow of the shell had become hard. A few air chambers, and the final living space at the top right of the shell, have been filled with a dark mass. As a result, the suture lines can be clearly seen. The suture lines mark the points where the chamber partitions were joined to the inside of the shell. Jurassic, 9 cm in diameter.

5

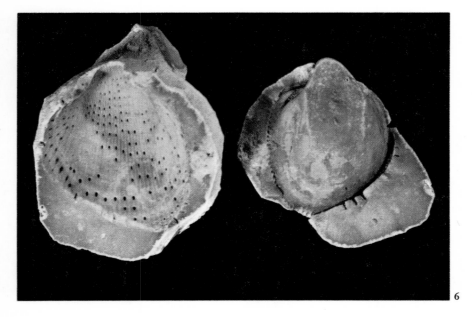

6

6. External and internal moulds of a cockle

On the left is the external mould, or imprint, which the shell left on the silt which surrounded it. The mould is hollow. The shell was spiny, and caused tiny holes in the mould. The shell itself has dissolved completely, and the fossil on the right is the internal mould of the same shell—the hardened remains of the silt which filled the shell. Cretaceous, 10 cm long.

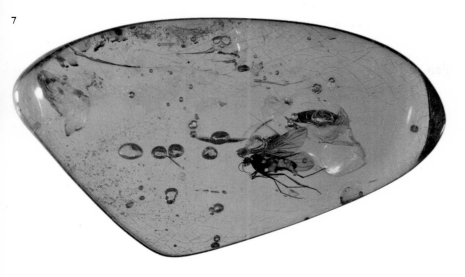

7

7. Insect in amber

Fossilised insects are not common. This little fly was caught and surrounded by a sticky resinous mass, which in time fossilised as amber. Nothing is left of the fly itself, but its imprint is seen in the amber. Tertiary, 3 cm across.

8. Footprints of birds

Any sign of ancient life preserved in stone is called a fossil, not just the actual remains. It is not always clear which animal made a particular footprint, or crawled, lay, dug or left droppings on the earth, but in this case it was definitely a bird, probably of a flamingo type. Tertiary, each footprint 10 cm across.

9. Fern on shale from a coal mine

The leaves were pressed flat and the softer parts disappeared completely. The mould, with a thin layer of coal, has been preserved. Carboniferous. The stone is about 16 cm across.

8

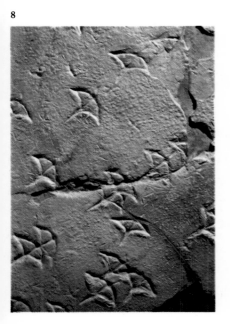

9

Cambrian

10. Trilobites

Trilobites have no living relatives. They became extinct towards the end of the Permian. They probably crawled over the sea-bed, because tracks have been found which must have been caused by them (11) but some species could probably float as well as crawl, and maybe even swim.

Nor do we know what trilobites ate. Probably they lived on algae, or on the organic materials present in the silt of the sea-bed, but they may have lived on dead animals.

We do know the stages of growth from larva to adult animal in several species, because the armour did not grow with the animal and had to be shed and replaced. It is possible to gather together many trilobite 'suits of armour' *(carapaces)* of the same species, put them in order, and study the stages of growth.

11. Track of crawling trilobite
Length of track 12 cm.

12. Trilobites in rock
Length of trilobites 2 cm.

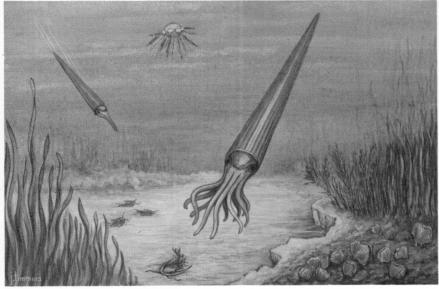

13

13. Nautiloids on the Ordovician sea bed

In the background is a floating colony of graptolites, and some brachiopods are clinging to the bottom in the right-hand foreground.

The one present-day nautiloid generally shoots itself backwards through the water by squirting water forwards. For a long time it was assumed that Ordovician nautiloids must have done likewise. But other living relatives of the nautiloids, the squid and octopus, can swim backwards or forwards as they please, and from fossil traces of the tentacles of nautiloids it seems likely that they could do the same.

14. Nautiloid shell

A section cut through a slightly crooked nautilus shell in limestone, showing the living compartments. About 20 cm long.

14

Silurian

15. Eurypterids

These were arthropods which belong to the same group as the spiders but which died out in the Permian. Some eurypterids grew to giant size compared with other arthropods—up to 3 metres long. They are sometimes called 'sea-scorpions', but though they are very distantly related to scorpions, and look rather like them, they mainly lived in fresh or brackish water and not in the sea. Their gills were well protected and they may even have been able to spend some time out of the water.

Most of the eurypterids lived in the mud and crawled around in search of food, but others were more streamlined, and probably used their legs to swim with. They had strong jaws and teeth, and could probably prey on animals with external skeletons.

Remains of eurypterids and the early armoured fish are found in the same deposits, so the eurypterids may also have eaten fish, especially since the fish had not then become fast swimmers and would not have been able to escape easily from their larger enemies.

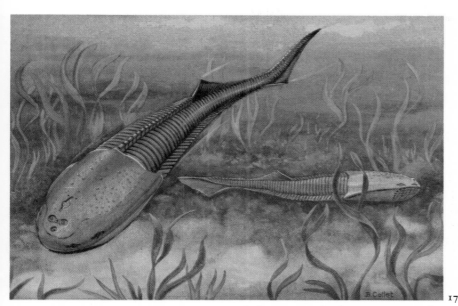

16. Graptolites

Graptolites were still common in the Silurian, especially forms which had only one row of tube-shaped cells arranged along a stick. This kind did not form large colonies. Length of sticks, 2·5 cm.

17. Jawless fishes

These are primitive forms of the earliest class of vertebrates. They were clumsy creatures compared with modern fish. If they were able to swim at all, they had little ability to steer or balance, being able to wriggle only the rear of their bodies. The front part was completely covered by a bony skeleton, and the rear part by scales. The head armour was at first joined to the body armour, so the head could not move independently at all, but forms soon developed where the head could be moved because the head and body armour were no longer joined. Later forms of jawless fish were also better balanced and could steer better, using fin-like extensions on the sides of their bodies.

The jawless fish probably spent much of their time on the bottom, filtering organic substances from the mud. The position of their eyes was also typical of bottom-dwellers—placed close together high on the head, looking upwards. Their length varied from about 10–20 cm.

It is interesting to note that the larval stage of the lamprey, a present-day jawless fish, is still a filter-feeder, though the adult lamprey has developed a special mouth for sucking blood.

In general, life is thought to have originated in the sea, and it was for a long time assumed that the first vertebrates lived in the sea and that later forms adapted to fresh water. But some scientists point out that Silurian and Devonian fish are rarely found in typical sea-sediments. They are much more common in deposits closer to the coast or in deltas or lagoons. Is it therefore more likely that the first vertebrates lived in fresh water? The controversy over this is still in full swing.

It is generally accepted, however, that the ancestors of the vertebrates were, rather surprisingly, a type of filter-feeding animal which burrowed into the mud on the bottom and waited for organic material to drift in, and that internal gills began as filters.

Devonian

19. An imprint of a Devonian plant

This is form D as shown in illustration 18. The stems branch into two equal parts and carry thornlike scale leaves. This piece of stone is about 5 cm in height.

18. Landscape at the beginning of the Devonian

Until the end of the Silurian there was no life on dry land. The first land plants we know of are from the late Silurian, and those are few and far between. But at the beginning of the Devonian, land plants began to spread. These plants were at first of a very primitive kind (types A–D in illustration 18). They reproduced by means of spores. Type D grew to about 50 cm tall. This primitive type of plant had no true leaves.

There were also ancestors of the lycopods or club-mosses, and the horsetails, forms E and F in the illustration. These plants were similar to their present-day descendants but they had thicker stems and fairly strong scale leaves. Their spore-carrying organs were not grouped into heads, and each was placed at the base of a scale leaf. Club-mosses and horsetails are now herbaceous plants only.

20. Freshwater fish

Armoured fish living on the bottom were able to move by crawling and sometimes swimming. The movable 'legs', made up from several plates, look rather like those of an arthropod. About 15 cm long.

Top left, a primitive brush-finned fish is swimming. The head was covered with bony plates, the body with scales. The short broad fins had a bony skeleton, which made it possible for their descendants to become land animals. These primitive fish became more or less extinct at the beginning of the Permian, and it caused great excitement when in 1938 a 'living fossil' coelacanth was caught off the coast of Africa.

A lungfish is swimming, top right. The present-day Australian lungfish is thought to be a direct descendant. Brush-finned fish and armoured fish all had lungs, and this allowed them to survive when the stagnant pools in which they lived dried up in summer.

21. Fossil armoured fish, of the type shown in (20)

10 cm long, found in the Orkneys.

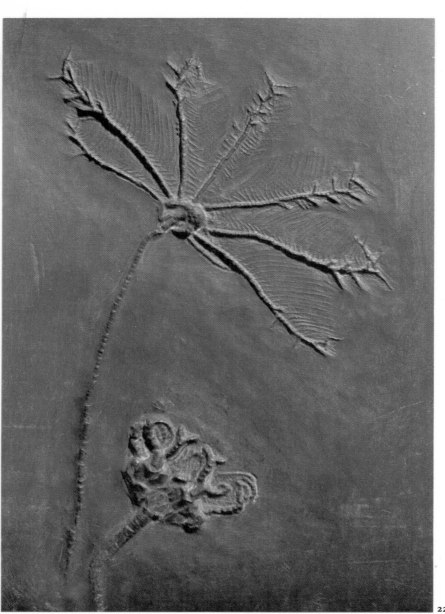

22

22. Skeleton of a sea-lily in shale

Sea-lilies (crinoids) are not plants but animals. Like starfish, which aren't stars, and sea cucumbers, which aren't cucumbers, sea-lilies are echinoderms — invertebrate animals living only in the seas.

The calcite skeleton of a sea-lily consists of a stem, which attaches it to the sea floor, a small body, and 'arms'. The stem is made of little discs, each with a hole in the middle through which ran a nerve. The body was protected by several closely fitting plates. The 'arms' were covered with cilia ('hairs') and were used to bring food to the mouth. The number of arms in early sea-lilies was five. Five is the typical number of arms in echinoderms. These arms sometimes branched, however, so that there may be more arms visible. This specimen has a span across the arms of 10 cm.

In recent years palaeontologists have been particularly interested in this kind of animal, because it now seems possible that they may have been quite closely related as 'cousins' to the earliest vertebrates, our own distant ancestors.

Carboniferous

23. Late Carboniferous landscape

Club-mosses occupied an important position among the plants, for they grew to the size of trees and much of the coal was formed from them. The leaves were long and fleshy, growing from the stem but falling off fairly soon and leaving a scar. Two main groups can be distinguished, mainly from the pattern of leaf scars. They may be either in vertical rows as in the tree on the left, called *Sigillaria* or be diamond shaped and occur in diagonal rows, as in the trees on the right *(Lepidodendron)*. Both these trees reached a height of 20–30 metres.

Horsetails were also quite common in Carboniferous forests (centre of picture). There are still herbaceous horsetails around today, some 400 million years after their first appearance.

24. Stem imprint of Sigillaria

In Latin *sigillum* means a seal. Each seal or leaf scar is 7 mm across.

25. Imprint of horsetail twigs in shale

Between 5 and 9 cm long.

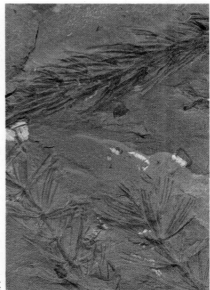

Permian

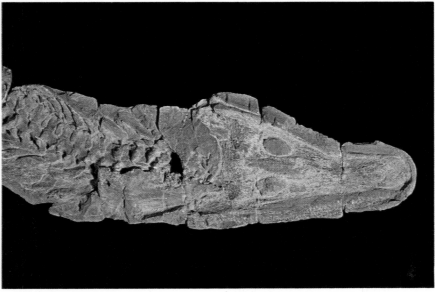

26. Permian landscape

In the foreground is an amphibian, behind it is a pelycosaur. The amphibians flourished in this period. The one illustrated was about 1·5 metres long and was one of the larger species. Its legs were sturdy, but it must have stayed near water because it lived on fish.

The pelycosaurs were important predators, hunting large fish, amphibians, and their own smaller relatives. The one illustrated was 3 metres long and had sharp teeth. The 'sail' on its back is supported by very tall vertebrae. It is thought that this may have been an early attempt to develop a mechanism for regulating temperature; the surface area could have absorbed heat. In this way the cold-blooded reptile would have been able to make better use of the heat of the sun.

Only a few of the mammal-like reptiles had this kind of sail. Another branch of mammal-like reptiles, the therapsids, may have developed constant body temperature.

27. Amphibian skull and vertebrae

Of the species shown in (26), lower foreground. Skull length 20 cm.

28. Shell eater from an inland sea

The shell-eaters occupy a special-ised place among the reptiles of the Triassic. Their teeth were entirely adapted to eating shellfish and snails: they had firm, forward-pointing incisors used to wrench loose shells fixed to the seabed or rocks, and large flat molars to crush and grind the hard shells. Often they lost teeth in the process, and loose molars are not uncommon in Triassic limestone.

The shell-eaters arose and became extinct during the Triassic. During that time there were plenty of shells. The animal illustrated lived in the mid-Triassic. It was about 2 metres long, had a massive skeleton with a flat belly armour formed by the ribs. With its long slender tail it must have been a good swimmer, and its front and hind legs were well developed for walking on land.

29. Sea-lily in limestone

The discs of the top of the stalk can be clearly seen; the part shown is 33 cm long.

30. Shell prints in limestone

Width of slab 12 cm. This type of rock, found in Germany, has so many shells that is locally known as 'musselchalk'.

29

→
30

Jurassic

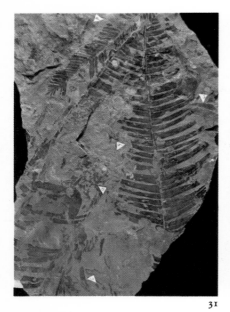

31. Leaf-print of a cycad

Plants of this type existed in great numbers and variety during the Mesozoic period (i.e. from the Triassic to the Cretaceous). They were dumpy trees, rather like palms (see the tree on the left in illustration 35). One species belonging to this group survives today. The large branch here is about 20 cm long.

32. Dragonfly

Delicate, perishable parts like the wings of a dragonfly are inevitably very rare as fossil finds. Only in very favourable circumstances will such brittle parts be preserved.

The rock from which this dragonfly comes, together with many other beautifully preserved fossils, is a finely grained limestone from Bavaria. It is known as lithographic limestone because it is suitable for making lithographs. It used to be quarried for that purpose at the town of Solenhafen; now it is mainly quarried for decorative tiles.

Many fossils emerged during quarrying operations, the most remarkable being that of the earliest known bird, *Archaeopteryx*. We should perhaps have thought this was a flying reptile if the Solenhafen limestone had not preserved impressions of its feathers. From this area there have also come skeletons of flying reptiles (pterosaurs) with the imprint of their flying membranes, jellyfish and insects. The wingspan of this dragonfly was about 20 cm.

33. Pterosaurs

Many types of flying reptile developed during the Mesozoic. The type illustrated, *Rhamphorhynchus,* had a very long skull and a long tail, with a kind of rudder at the end of it. Its wing construction, with a greatly extended fourth finger supporting the membrane, seems particularly suitable for gliding. But the membrane was very easily torn and even slight damage would have made it impossible to fly. It is not clear how these pterosaurs moved when not flying. Their skeletons made it almost impossible to walk on two legs or four. But they must have been able to move about if only to prepare for the next flight.

33 B.Collet

The skin of the pterosaurs was covered not with scales but with something like hair, and they may have been able to keep their body temperature almost constant.

Rhamphorhynchus (the name means 'prow-beak') had sharp teeth and lived on fish, probably diving out of the air into the water for them. It flourished during the Jurassic and had a wingspan of about a metre. During the Cretaceous there were pterosaurs such as *Pteranodon* with wingspans of 8 metres, but there were also smaller types such as *Pterodactylus,* the size of a sparrow.

34. Bony fish

These are boned fish of the ray-finned type—the type to which most of our modern fish belong. The fish illustrated are sometimes referred to as 'fossil sprats'. They and their relations can be considered as the ancestors of modern fish. The rock is the Solenhafen lithographic limestone; each fish is about 5 cm long.

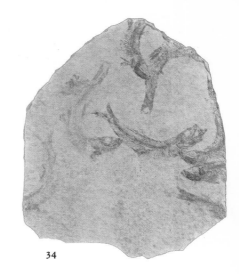

34

B. Collet

35

35. Brontosaurus and Stegosaurus

This is a late Jurassic landscape, with a cycad tree on the left (see page 38). The *Brontosaurus,* seen standing in water, weighed about 35 tons; his relative *Brachiosaurus* reached 50 tons. Huge animals like these lasted right through the Mesozoic.

Brontosaurus and *Stegosaurus* were both plant-eaters. They had heavy bodies on massive legs, broad feet, and a long tail. The comparatively small head had weak jaws and it is surprising that they were able to eat enough to keep such huge bodies going. The front legs, especially in *Stego-saurus,* are shorter than the hind legs. It is probable that their ancestors walked on two legs and were predators, and that they went back to four legs when they became plant-eaters.

Brontosaurus and *Stegosaurus* were still around in the Cretaceous. It is almost certain that their legs, though sturdy, could only just move the mighty body around. *Brontosaurus* and similar forms probably spent most of their lives in lakes or marshes, where the water supported some of the body-weight.

Stegosaurus was about 6 metres long, which is small compared to a 20 metre *Brontosaurus*. Being smaller and spending its time on land, it must have been an easier prey for a large dinosaur, but it was not defenceless. There were two rows of bony plates on its back and fearsome spikes on its tail.

36. A horned dinosaur and a predator dinosaur

The horned dinosaurs did not last very long—only 35 million years, compared with about 130 million years for the predator dinosaurs. They were plant-eaters, but better able to defend themselves than the *Stegosaurus* which became extinct early in the Cretaceous. The horned dinosaurs were well protected round the neck by a bony collar; most predators seized their prey by the neck (they still do) and the combination of bony collar and vicious horns must have deterred

36

them. The form illustrated reached about 6 metres in length, and the horn on its nose was 50 cm long.

The predator illustrated is a smaller relative of the famous *Tyrannosaurus rex*. This form was about 9 metres long, whereas *Tyrannosaurus rex,* the largest land predator of all time, was 15 metres. The front legs seem absurdly small in relation to the body and tail. They are too weak to hold prey, and cannot even reach the mouth. Later species had even feebler front legs, so probably these legs had no real function.

It is now thought that these huge meat-eaters may not have been such active predators after all. Their teeth are certainly those of flesh-eaters, but perhaps they lived mainly on carcasses they had not killed.

3

37. Mosasaurus

These lived in the seas of the late Cretaceous, and were found throughout the world. The first fossil of this kind was found near the River Meuse in the Netherlands. The chalk there has been quarried for centuries. The skull of this unknown reptile was more than a metre long. It was named a Meuse-reptile (the Latin name for the Meuse was *Mosa*) and it attracted many admiring tourists. It became so famous that when the French army entered Maastricht in 1795 they had special instructions to search out the skull and take it to Paris. This they did, and the skull is still there.

Since then, further remains have been found, and we now know what the complete animal looked like. They were lizards adapted to life in sea water, and the largest forms could be 15 metres long. They had a flexible tail for swimming, and the legs served mainly for steering. They lived on fish.

Mosasaurus appeared during the Cretaceous and became extinct, like so many other reptiles at the end of that period. Its remains are found in chalk all over the world, in England, in New Zealand, in Kansas, USA.

38. Vertebrae of a Mosasaurus

The main part of each vertebra, excluding the spines, is about 5–6 cm across.

39. Internal mould of an ammonite

This can be recognised as a mould from a straight-shelled ammonite because of the suture lines. It is 37 cm long. Ammonites were flourishing throughout the Cretaceous; they vanished suddenly at the end of that period.

38

39

40. Fish in limestone

A fine example of a bony fish of the ray-finned modern type, from the Tertiary. The ray-finned fish went through a rapid process of development at the beginning of this period. This specimen is 20 cm long.

41. Skeleton of a frog

Frogs are one of the few groups of amphibians alive today. They have a long fossil history: in the Jurassic there were already frogs which looked almost exactly like the frogs we know today. The form has survived for almost 190 million years, despite the great changes which have occurred in the world during that time. The frogs must always have found an environment in which they could thrive.

The origins of the frog are still a mystery. We do not know from which group of amphibians they are descended. The earliest frog found so far is from the Triassic, but it was already quite close to the modern form, though less well developed for hopping.

The distance from head to toe in this fossil is 13 cm.

41

42

was when *Brontotherium* died out.

Drastic changes were necessary before the forest animal could live on the plains; it evolved into a fast runner with strong legs, and teeth which could chew the tough grasses.

The most striking changes in the evolution of the horse are:

increase in size (although this was not consistent)
changes in teeth
stronger legs
growth of the middle toe
reduced size of the other two toes

42. Brontotherium

Brontotherium was an 'odd-toed ungulate', and was descended from the same ancestors as the horse. The development of the odd-toed ungulates (they have one, three, or five toes in their hoof) was mainly a matter of getting bigger. *Brontotherium* had a shoulder height of 2·40 metres. Unlike horses, they never developed a good set of teeth, and this is probably why they are extinct. Their teeth were only suitable for soft plant food, and any change of climate, bringing a change in vegetation, could have been fatal.

We don't know why they had horns on the head, but there seems to be a difference in the size of horn between males and females.

43. Family tree of the horse

Even this simplified family tree shows that the evolution of the horse has been far from consistent. The 'first horse', *Eohippus,* was a small animal with delicate legs which lived in tropical forests. Its teeth were weak, and only suitable for the juicy plant food it found in the forest. During the Tertiary the climate worsened and the forests gradually disappeared and gave way to vast plains with dry grasses. This

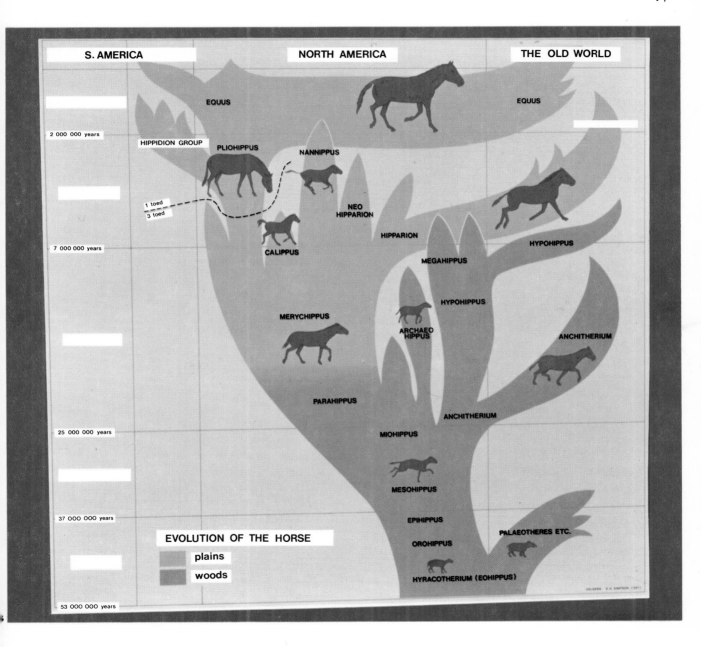

EVOLUTION OF THE HORSE

Quaternary

jan timmers '71

44. Woolly-haired mammoth

This animal is not known from fossils alone: there are cave paintings of it made by men in the Old Stone Age, and there have also been complete carcasses found, frozen solid in the soil of Siberia. The carcasses showed how the mammoth had protected itself against the cold with a thick layer of fat and a dense coat of hair. The longest hairs, on the back and sides, were 50 cm long.

It was possible to examine the stomachs and to discover that these animals ate grass. Surprisingly, the species of grasses proved that the climate in Siberia at that time was warmer than it is now. Probably the mammoths lived on in Siberia after the last Ice Age, when they had already become extinct elsewhere. The number of carcasses in Siberia must have been great, for the inhabitants have traded in ivory from the tusks since time immemorial.

A mammoth drawn in earth, found in a cave at Arcu-sur-Cure, 60 cm across

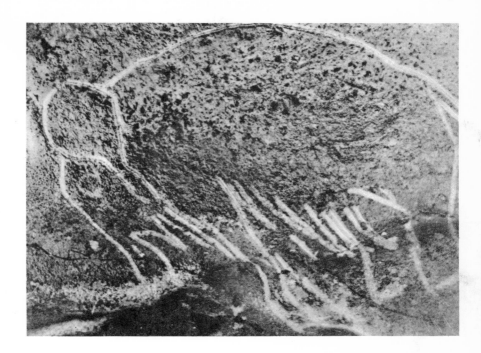

Two drawings of mammoths found in caves at Bernifal, length about 70 cm

Stages in the development of man

Until recently it was thought that the humanoid primates which have lived during the last two million years belonged to many different genera. Almost every new find was given a new name. But as the finds increased in number, it became possible to analyse them more thoroughly It appeared that there were not many different kinds after all, and the number of genera could be reduced to two—*Australopithecus* (which means 'southern ape-man') and *Homo*.

Australopithecus lived from abou[t] 2 500 000 to 500 000 years ag[e] Most finds come from Africa.

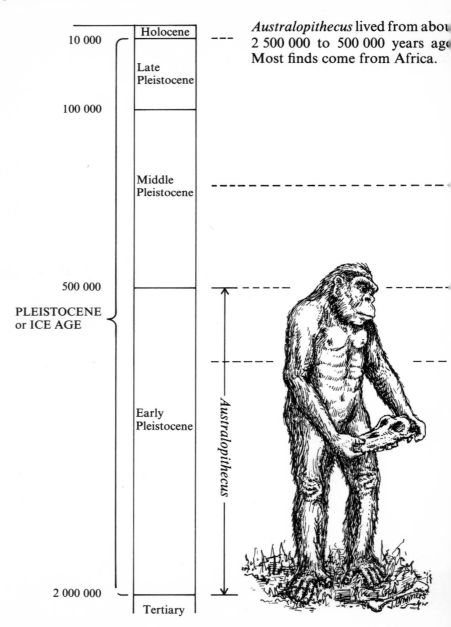

10 000	Holocene
	Late Pleistocene
100 000	
	Middle Pleistocene
500 000	
PLEISTOCENE or ICE AGE	Early Pleistocene
2 000 000	
	Tertiary

Australopithecus

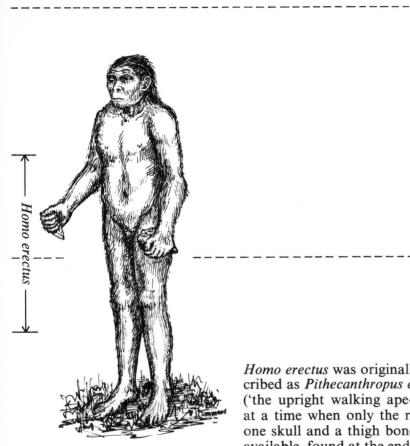

Homo erectus was originally described as *Pithecanthropus erectus* ('the upright walking ape-man') at a time when only the roof of one skull and a thigh bone were available, found at the end of the last century in Java. From later finds it seems that this kind of man was widely found over Asia, Europe and Africa from about 700 000 to about 200 000 years ago.

Neanderthal man was a form of *Homo sapiens*—our own species. The genus *Homo* evolved about 500 000 years ago. They are called by this name because the first skull of this kind was found in the Neander valley near Dusseldorf in Germany.

Plants and animals mentioned in this book

PLANTS

Bacteria

Algae

Vascular plants

Spore plants ....
{ primitive plants
club-mosses
horsetails
ferns }

Seed plants ....
{
gymnosperms .... { seed ferns
cycads
conifers }

angiosperms........................... { grasses
trees }
}

ANIMALS

Invertebrates ....
{
sponges
jellyfish, corals
worms
moss-animalcules
brachiopods
molluscs .... { shellfish
snails
cephalopods ...... { nautiloids
ammonites
octopus
squid } }

arthropods............................. { trilobites
crayfish
insects
spiders and scorpions }

echinoderms .... { starfish
sea lilies
sea urchins }

graptolites
}

Vertebrates.............................
{ fish
amphibians
reptiles
birds
mammals }

Other books about prehistoric animals and man

Animals before Adam, W E Swinton (Dent)

Dinosaurs, W E Swinton (British Museum, Natural History)

Fossils, H. H. Swinnerton (Collins, New Naturalist Series)

Fossil amphibians and reptiles, W E Swinton (British Museum, Natural History)

Fossil birds, W E Swinton (British Museum, Natural History)

History of the primates, Sir W E LeGros Clark (British Museum, Natural History)

Introduction to palaeontology, A Morley Davies (Allen & Unwin)

Life before man, the story of fossils, Duncan Forbes (A & C Black)

Man and the vertebrates, A S Romer (Penguin)

Man the tool-maker, K P Oakley (British Museum, Natural History)

Outline of palaeontology, H H Swinnerton (Edward Arnold)

Prehistoric animals, Barry Cox (Hamlyn all-colour paperbacks)

Succession of life through geological time, K P Oakley and H M Muir-Wood (British Museum, Natural History)

Theory of evolution, J Maynard Smith (Penguin)

Black's Picture Information Book Series

1. Insects — Matthew Prior
2. Pond and marsh — James Whinray
3. Seashore — Ian Murray
4. Trees — Clare Williams
5. Conservation — James Whinray
6. Flowers and their visitors — Janet Davidson
7. Fungi — George Parkinson
8. Pests — Matthew Prior
9. Animals and plants in the fields — Valerie Duncan
10. Mountains, plains and rivers — Robert Webb
11. Prehistoric animals — David Seymour
12. What you can find in a park — Clare Williams

Index